Deep

By Stephen Rickard

ıshed in 2026 by
ᵥwood House Press
‡ Clinton Street
lo, NY 14224

ed in the United States of America

Library of Congress Cataloging-in-Publication Data:
Names: Rickard, Stephen, 1957-, author.
Title: Deep ; We Need to Win / written by Stephen Rickard.
Description: Buffalo, NY : Norwood House Press, 2026. | Series: Phonics all-stars: phase 3 |
Identifiers: ISBN 9781978577961 (pbk.) | ISBN 9781978577978 (library bound) | ISBN 9781978577985 (ebook)
Subjects: LCSH: Reading–Phonetic method–Juvenile literature. | English language–Phonetics–Juvenile literature. | Underwater exploration–Juvenile literature. | Deep-sea animals–Juvenile literature. | Sportsmanship–Juvenile literature.
Classification: LCC LB1573.3 R534 2026 | DDC 372.465–dc23

CPSIA compliance information: Batch #CW26NHP: For further information contact Norwood House Press at 1-800-237-9932.

This sub can go deep.

It can go deep, deep, deep.

This is a sub as well.

This sub is a bot.
It has no man in it.

In the deep, this bot sub can see things that a sub with a man cannot see.

You can see lots of odd things in the deeps.

You need to wait a bit.
Then you will see them.

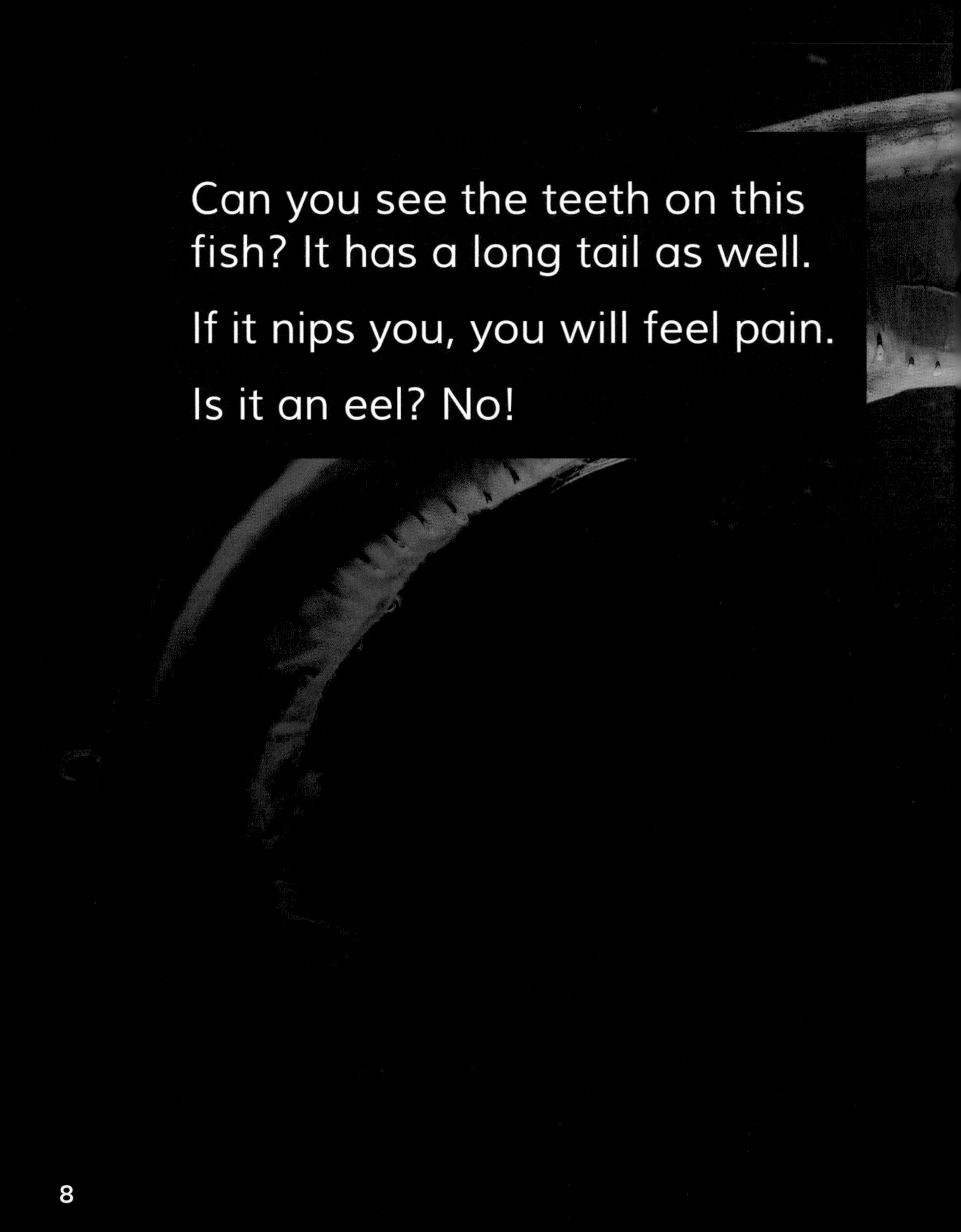

Can you see the teeth on this fish? It has a long tail as well.

If it nips you, you will feel pain.

Is it an eel? No!

Is that an odd fish?

No, it is a bag.

In the deeps, a shell fish waits in the weeds.

Can you see it?

You can go into the deeps as well.

We Need to Win

By Stephen Rickard

Jeff sails in his boat.

He needs to win.

He aims to keep the quick boats in sight.

4577

4577
5569

Gail runs in the rain.

She needs to win.

In the rain, she will get wet feet.

Gail cannot jog. To win, she will need to be quick on the road.

The boat on the right,
the red boat, needs to win.

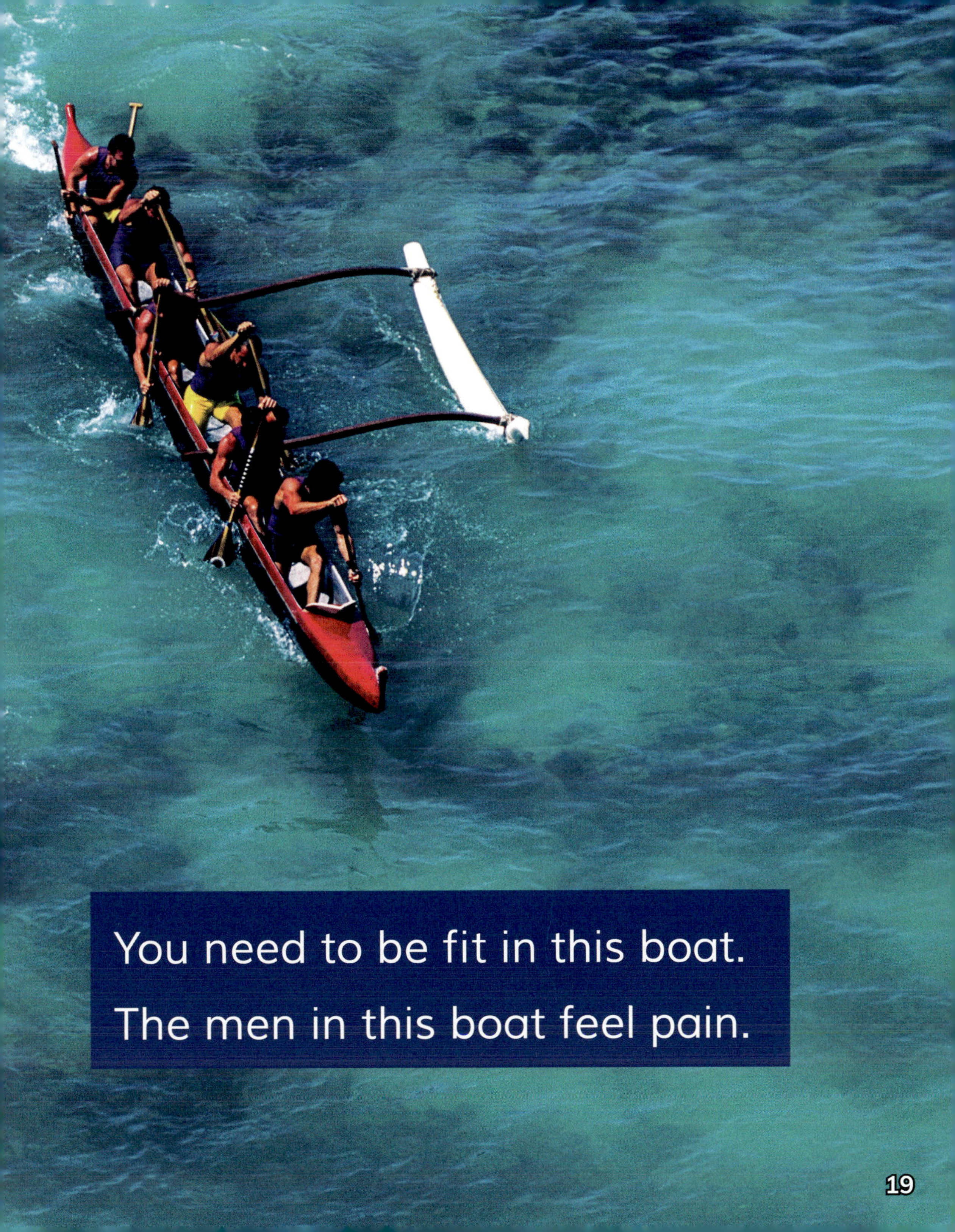

You need to be fit in this boat.

The men in this boat feel pain.

Kev hangs on the rings.
He needs to win.

He keeps his legs up high.
Will he let go?

Bob and Kim need to win.

Bob and Kim will not get wet, will not need to rush, and will not feel pain.

Kim gets the goal that wins.

Kim tells Bob, "You see, I was right. We ***did*** win."